Self Discovery

Self Discovery

Prose and Poems: A Journey from Pain to Purpose

Lisa C. Williams

Writers Club Press
San Jose New York Lincoln Shanghai

Self Discovery
Prose and Poems: A Journey from Pain to Purpose

All Rights Reserved © 2002 by Lisa C. Williams

No part of this book may be reproduced or transmitted in any form or by any means, graphic, electronic, or mechanical, including photocopying, recording, taping, or by any information storage retrieval system, without the permission in writing from the publisher.

Writers Club Press
an imprint of iUniverse.com, Inc.

For information address:
iUniverse.com, Inc.
5220 S 16th, Ste. 200
Lincoln, NE 68512
www.iuniverse.com

All rights reserved. Scripture quotations are taken from the Holy Bible, New Living Translation, copyright ©1996. Used by permission of Tyndale House Publishers, Inc., Wheaton, Illinois 60189. All rights reserved. "Self Discovery Affirmation" and "Two Sisters" by Rita Loyd. Used by permission of Nurturing Art, Huntsville, Alabama. The epigraph opening poem excerpt is from "What I Live For" by George Linnaeus Banks, the nineteenth-century poet.
Cover artwork by Rita Loyd (www.nurturingart.com).
This is in part a work of fiction. Although inspired by actual events, the names, persons, places, and characters are inventions of the author. Any resemblance to people living or deceased is purely coincidental.

ISBN: 0-595-20162-8

Printed in the United States of America

Dedication

I dedicate this book to my best friend and husband, Lynn Calvo. Your prayers and gentleness encouraged my soul and spirit for the journey of self discovery. Your acceptance of all and who I am have often been more than I or others could handle. Never once did you flinch or retreat from my uncovered pain, anguish, and terrifying nightmares to a place of comfort. Husband, your continuing flow of support and love provided the necessary nourishment for my soul while on its journey and during its recovery. Your daily prayers along with mine provided the balm for my healing. I count it a joy and privilege to live in God's comfort today! I count it a blessing to have you as my best friend and husband.

Thank you for allowing God to direct your words, touch, and footsteps for these past fourteen years. I honor God for all of the discoveries, my healing, and our friendship, partnership, awesome marriage, and children!

Lovingly,
Lisa

Epigraph

I live for those who love me,
    Whose hearts are kind and true;
For the Heaven that smiles above me,
    And awaits my spirit too;
For all human ties that bind me,
For the task by God assigned me,
For the bright hopes yet to find me,
    And the good that I can do.

I live to hold communion
    With all that is divine,
To feel there is a union
    'Twixt Nature's heart and mine;
To profit by affliction,
Reap truth from fields of fiction,
Grow wiser from conviction,
    And fulfil God's grand design.

I live for those who love me,
    For those who know me true,
For the Heaven that smiles above me,
    And awaits my spirit too;
For the cause that lacks assistance,

Self Discovery

For the wrong that needs resistance,
For the future in the distance,
    And the good that I can do.

—excerpted from "What I live for" by George Linnaeus Banks

Contents

Chapter 1 Stolen Innocents 1
   Self Discovery 1
   On My Own 2
   Whispers of Truth 3
   Speak 3
   I Hid 3
   His Belt 4
   Taken 5
   Raped 6
   This Glorious Weight 6
   Turn Off the Silence 6
   I Feel 7
   Sweet Zoë 8
   Twenty Years 8
   Death 11

Chapter 2 Solicitation 12
   Old Man Rivers : In His White Eldorado 12
   Money for My Honey 13
   The Reverend 13
   No Beds Allowed 14
   No Longer 15
   Purposed 15

Self Discovery

Chapter 3 Subjugation	16
SisterFriend	*16*
Move On	*16*
Worthy	*17*
No More Light	*18*
No More Shade	*19*
Killed by Love	*20*
Truth	*21*

Chapter 4 Façade	22
Mask	*22*
Stepping Stones	*23*
Hidden Rubies	*23*
Undress	*23*
Once More	*23*
Where is My God?	*24*
Stand	*24*
Healing	*24*
Freedom	*24*
Stand	*25*
Beginning in the End	*25*

Chapter 5 Saved	26
Travel	*26*
Check Your Time	*26*
God	*27*
Birth	*28*
Choose Life	*28*
God's ABC	*28*
Comfort	*29*
Life is…	*30*

Assurance 31
Unity 31
Focus 31

Chapter 6   Praise 32
My Daily Prayer 32
Enlightenment 33
Powerless 33
My Savior! 33
Points of Entry 34
Emancipation 35
Your Debt 35
The Answer 36
Nightly Prayer 36

Chapter 7   Melody 38
Spirituals 38
Grace and Mercy 38
It Is Well 39
My Soul 39
If I Can Help Some Woman 40
Carolyn's Song 40
When She Sings 41

Chapter 8   Kindred 42
Marriage 42
Husband 42
Laugh Out Loud 43
Linkage 43
Essence of Life 43
Paul, the Laughter in My Soul 43

Self Discovery

    Joseph, My Joy 44
    Why 44
    Rest 45

Chapter 9   Friends 46
    Friend 46
    She Knows Me 46
    Two Sisters 47
    Two Sisters, Part II 47
    Unhealthy 47

Chapter 10 Identity 48
    Pureness of Love 48
    Hues of Skin 48
    Little Black Dress 49
    Black Hair 49

Chapter 11 Self 50
    Celebrating Life 50
    Celebration 50
    Self Trust 51
    Peace 51
    Self Discovery Affirmation 51
    Standing In the Gap 52
    My Vow 53
    Discovery of Self 53

Appendix A: Purposeful Scriptures 59
    What to do when you are: 60
       Afraid 60
       Angry 62
       Unsure About God 64

Ashamed 67
Having Doubts About Yourself 67
What to do when you are feeling: 69
   Guilty 69
   Confused 70
   Worried 71
   Stressed & Anxious 73
   Lonely 75
   Discouraged 76
What to do when you: 78
   Feel everything is going wrong in your life 78
   Are Deserted by friends and family 79
   Are Facing Trying circumstances 80
   Want to forgive 81
   Want to live as God would have it 83

Appendix B: Learned Lessons 87
   Getting Your Priorities Straight 87
   Attitude is Everything 88
   Improving Behavior 88
   Trusting God 89
   Living Your Purpose 89
   Leaning on Faith 90

Appendix C: Resources For Healing the Hurt 91

Foreword

In Self Discovery, Poet Lisa C. Williams excavates the painful memories and aftermath of childhood incest and violence. Through self examination, Lisa pieces together for the reader the process she took to find peace and healing in God's Love.

I consider Lisa a dear friend and a sister. Her light shines bright in my life and in the lives of those destined to learn from her. Lisa boldly states her truth in this book, encouraging others to step outside their own dark shadows in order to reclaim and embrace their true beauty that lies deep within.

Friend and Sister,
Rita Loyd

I met Lisa Williams just over twenty years ago through a mutual business partner. We just clicked, both of us having experienced much of what life had to offer at an extremely young age. The realization that we were then and still are now on a path that has twisted, turned, crossed, and forever linked us has forged a bond with Lisa which combines the best of sisterhood and friendship.

I am deeply honored that she has asked me to comment and be a part of this extraordinary book. I know that all of you will be warmed with Lisa's extreme joy and generosity of spirit. But be forewarned: it is highly contagious! Everything happens for a reason, and I know that we

Self Discovery

are still on the path. I am awed by the person she was then as well as the person she has become—with a little help from her friends!!

In friendship and sisterhood,
Soluria Galloway Pearson

Preface

Most Holy God, I glorify Your name and praise You for who You are and what You have done. You alone are holy and worthy of the highest praise. I honor You as the true and living God with all my heart, soul, mind and strength.

O, Gracious Lord, please shower Your grace on those I love who struggle with sin, who are broken by life's problems, plagued by disease, and caught in trying circumstances. I pledge to minister to their needs as I ask You to comfort, heal, strengthen, and mend in ways my words and deeds cannot.

Lord, thank You for hearing not only the prayer of my words, but the prayer of my heart. Be exalted in my life as I thank You for Your grace and mercy.

Through the power of the Holy Spirit and by the grace of Jesus, I offer this prayer. Amen

Acknowledgements

I give thanks:

To my love, my husband, Lynn Calvo, who is my mentor and best friend. To my sons, Paul, Joseph, Andrew, and my daughters, Mia and Ashlyn, for graciously sharing me with others so that they may walk their path to healing.

To Mrs. Glenda Robinson, who stood in the gap with her husband, Walter, for my sanity and my son Joseph's birth. I will forever honor your resolve and submission to the will of God. Thank you for securing Joseph's precious gift of life for me and the world to experience. I miss you so terribly, but I rejoice in knowing that God now holds you in His gentle hands.

To these mature women of wisdom: Sallie Abbas, Laura Hilton, Dr. Johnnie Miles, Audrey Person, and Ann Smith, for their encouragement and demonstrated attitude of excellence.

To my circle of friends: Soluria Pearson, Carol Jones Hunter, Carolyn Sampson, Sharon Cox, Lorraine Stephens, Rita Loyd and Jackie Goodwyn for their creative labor and for contributing to my family's daily joy.

To these editors: Carol Hunter, The Creative Consultants for asking the right questions and providing editorial services. Sam Zahran for his painstaking proofreading and editorial advice and encouragement.

List of Contributors

Book Cover Painting "Self Discovery," done by watercolorist Rita Loyd. Please visit her web site at **http://www.nurturingart.com**.

Thanks to Carol Hunter, The Creative Consultants and Sam Zahran, for their editorial services.

Introduction

Self Discovery Prose and Poems: A Journey from Pain to Purpose creatively explores the process of releasing pain that is robbing us of joy in life. In letting go of the pain that may be a result of suffering or abuse, we become acquainted with and explore the heart and mind of the beautiful person that lives inside of our soul. Through the prose and poems in this book you'll embark on a truth seeking—journey that requires introspection, compassion and forgiveness. It is sometimes a painful process in itself, but a necessary part of growth, discovery and ultimately, peace and joy.

My Beautiful Sisters, self-discovery isn't only about you, but also about the other lives you've touched and will touch by knowing yourself intimately and living your truth. The very act of us looking deep and wide into our hidden pain means that one—day soon we will indeed heal the hurt and experience the freedom to celebrate life.

Discovering Self,
Lisa C. Williams

Chapter 1
Stolen Innocents

Self Discovery

It's frightening to think of gazing into the mirror.
Who might I see, who might I see?
It's terrifying to lift my face in front of the mirror.
Who will I see, who will I see?
It's paralyzing to open my eyes in the mirror.
Who might I be, who might I be?
My Lord, strengthen me, because today I'm ready for self discovery by looking into the mirror.

I am personally acquainted with the secrets that are kept hidden inside; yes, there are many hidden secrets that have died inside.

Please, Lord, strengthen me, for I'm afraid of just who I might see, just who I might see.

But I know if I'm ever to be set free, I must find the courage that too resides in me, so that I may earnestly look deep and wide at all that's hidden inside.

So please, Lord, stay near to me, for still I'm ashamed of what I might see, of what I might see during my self discovery.

Self Discovery

On My Own

I was very young when I left home, forced out on my own. My mother did not protect me; she just said it had to be.

Her words were bold, and extremely cold: "Daughter of twelve, you now must go, simply stated, you're destroying the family mold, and just so you know, your worth was never measured in gold."

She had chosen her mate over her daughter, the same mate who openly walked into her daughter's room during the late night, Yes, you guessed right: it was no longer just her mate that I had grown to hate.

I wondered how this could be, and why me, my body, was present for all his perverted meetings, and I stood without crying during those naked beatings.

And when night would fall, in would crawl his shadow shape, to force upon me the act of rape. While committing his crime, he whispered through his teeth that I should be kind and learn to mind.

In my silence I would cry, only to have him push harder inside, and say don't be shy. My, oh my, what a price I pay, just to keep death at bay.

Maybe, just maybe being abandoned at twelve is a blessing. At least her husband is no longer messing.

On my own, on my own, Oh Lord, I'm twelve and on my own.

Lisa C. Williams

Whispers of Truth

I hear whispers of truth, but not full thoughts;
I hear whispers of truth, but not full sentences;
I hear whispers of truth, but not full lines;
I hear whispers of truth, but not full with rhyme;
I hear whispers of truth, but not full and kind;
I hear whispers of truth, but not full—they're just mine;
I hear whispers of truth, but not full with sweet lines—they're just plainly mine.
Please, Madam, I'll take my whispers of truth full, with a slice of lime.

Speak

Speak your truth even when your voice is *shaky*.

Inspired by Diana Calvo Slater • I love you my sister.

I Hid

I hid because the knocks were too violent.
I hid because the harshness of words was too pounding.
I hid because the sound of laughter was too frightening.
I hid because the smiles were warnings.
I hid because the echo of quietness was much too loud.
I hid because the cries from myself were howling in their silence.
In the attic I hid, even when I was no longer a kid.

His Belt

I'm late, and my date, well, he's my aunt's lifelong mate.

I know for sure who it was, but it's not the family buzz.

I told him, and now he thinks he's on the limb. But I'm the one who's no longer innocent and slim.

Professing to be God-fearing, while all along adjusting his eyes for leering,

He leered and touched, and touched me much.

I was only five, and not yet alive, but now at fourteen, I'm experiencing pain I should not have seen.

The table is cold, and I'm just a child that's not so bold; Oh, Lord, why do these relatives scold?

As I lay, I tried to keep the doctor at bay, but soon realize that there was no more to say.

The child was ripped quickly from my soul, leaving me nothing to hold. Help me, for I am cold.

The thoughts and actions did linger long, among them—no, just with me, for I was left all alone and cold, just me and my moans.

How could this happen? How could they just leave me, to be?

Was I to blame, because this uncle came, deep into my room for nine years to play his game?

My mother said no, but I didn't know.

The shame, the shame, of this uncle's ugly game.

Why not jail, with denied bail?

In short order I lost all hope, but quickly found my comfort in dope. And soon like a pro I learned to smoke, without the choke.

Many years since have passed, and at last, by God's grace, I've managed to win a part of the race.

I'm no longer considered a hopeless drug case.

Lisa C. Williams

Even today with my strong religious base, a clean and sober face, I still haven't moved from that painful place. I've learned to cope without the dope.

But not how to cope without the shame, and pain? There is no measurable gain, while my soul is living in pain.

Grown now, I find that I'm still gagged and bound, because of the family I still silence the sound of my pain and the shame and the aloneness I've found.

My aunt stayed married to this man, forgiving and forgetting that he was by force my first man.

Lord, help me. Please, I need help, before I hang myself with his belt.

Inspired by Valeria Brown a woman who experienced incest as a child.

Taken

That I was taken out of the womb,
I thank You!
That I was taken out of my bed of innocence,
I despise You!
That I was taken out of my childhood and abused,
I curse You!
That I was taken out of my house of terror,
I bless You!
That I was taken out of my bondage and made whole,
I praise You!

Inspired by a woman who too was a child of incest

Raped

I was raped, I was raped again, again I was raped. My Lord, when will my rape end?

Surely my death would be a blessing, for I can no longer live with the indescribable pain of being raped, again and again.

Inspired by—too many women to mention by name

This Glorious Weight

This glorious weight is not because I can't control my eating;
This glorious weight is not because I don't exercise daily;
This glorious weight is not because I won't make up my mind to shed it;
This glorious weight is my protection;
This glorious weight is my comfort;
This glorious weight is my sanctity, for it keeps the men away, far, far, away.

Turn Off the Silence

The silence of fear, hate, isolation, child abuse, and forced silence is much too loud.

How do I turn it off?

The silence of domestic violence, hospital visits, makeup cover-ups, mental anguish, and excuses is much too loud.

How do I turn it off?

The silence of rape, incest, molestation, sodomy, guilt, and shame is much too loud.

How do I turn it off?

The silence of anxiety, confusion, depression, and rejection is much too loud.

How do I turn if off?

The silence of self-doubt, self-destruction, self-imprisonment, and embarrassment is much too loud.

How do I turn if off?

I need help to turn it off. Please help me turn it off. If you can hear me through my silence, please help me turn it off.

I Feel

I'm eight not fully developed, but this thing within—I have enveloped. My stomach has a rounded bend, but still they say my body is on the mend.

I feel thankful…

You can relax my dear, for that ugly period of strife in your life has come to an end, no longer will you need to fend off your first cousin.

I feel grateful…

Today the tearful lady said, my sweet child—you will birth your once removed kin. Lord, I don't understand except to say I must have sinned.

I feel shameful…

Inspired by a sister friend

Sweet Zoë

    My sweet Savior, my sweet Zoë.
    I did not give existence to the commissioned life You gave me.
    My sweet Savior, my sweet Zoë.
    I had the constitution of life ripped from my body in hopes of saving me.
    My sweet Savior, my sweet Zoë.
    I thought then it had to be, in order to preserve what was left of me.
    My sweet Savior, my sweet Zoë.
    Please forgive me, for what if she were me.

Inspired by Soluria Pearson and Karen Burke: you both are givers of life.

Twenty Years

    It hurts so bad inside, but my anguish and pain I have disguised.
    Intent on not losing control, I resolved that no one was to know.
    So morning after morning I dawn the smiling face, just to stay (why, I don't know) in the human race.
    For twenty years I sold myself a high priced lie, that eventually my plastic face would die.
    Yesteryear, I affirmed in my soul, that I would never again have to brave another winters night's cold.
    But to my surprise, it happened again, right before my very eyes.

My shelter search began, oh, Lord, why me; this time who knows where or how I'll be?

The overwhelming memories and pain left me dressed in shame; was I to blame? Too many thoughts at one time came; what else could this be except a game to render me insane. Who I'm I kidding? No one is bidding.

This time it was all too much for me, so I begged God: just let me leave.

I resolved in my soul that there would be no more begging, no, not for me.

That was easy to proclaim; I didn't even want to live and I certainly had no more to give.

So when and to whom did I bow down and allow to beat me about my head, just to have an uncomfortable bed?

I awoke in my car, out of gas, out of food, out of faith, and out of hope, but I don't smoke dope (I'm crazy enough, can you imagine something else besides me in me, anyway?)

I thought that God was like all the rest and that He too had left me hmm—at my best.

How much longer must I suffer for my sins, and the sins of others? I can no longer see the Bible's righteous guidelines. Church sister, there's no need to fast, pray, and bind for the sake of my mind. There is no saving my kind.

But still I'm asking, where are you God, where are You? You promised long ago that You would not leave, but I no longer can believe.

Where are you God, where are You? Do you pleasure in my poor measure? If not, then where is my promised treasure?

Then hope walked in—And in that very still moment deep within me, the Lord spoke, "I was waiting for you to become 'broken.'"

Self Discovery

God proceeded to say that I was never left unattended, but it was I who had pulled far away from the Light.

And within the same still moment, God took my hand in the darkness and guided me back to the Light.

The Lord saw that I was hungry and fed me the Word. I was thirsty, and God provided me a refreshing drink from Jesus' life. I was undressed and cold and was given the Holy Spirit to clothe and warm me.

God had never left me, but patiently waited for me, just to be, just to be still? until.

It wasn't until I was still, and in my broken place, that I was able to understand my case.

During that self discovery I moaned and sobbed every passing hour for days, while His grace and mercy provided me the cleansing shower, so that I could see, all that He wanted me to believe.

I learned that all my hurts and pains from yesterday would be healed, as I allowed His love to be revealed.

Twenty years of inner hurt and pain did heal when my secrets were undressed and revealed.

There in my broken place I realized the total cost of God's saving grace.

It was when the secrets were unearthed that God restored and gave me a new and joyous birth!

Inspired by the artwork of Rita Loyd and the raw emotions of Joanne Davis.

Death

Darkness is unacceptable for it smothers and strangles the seed of life.

Chapter 2
Solicitation

Old Man Rivers : In His White Eldorado

Old Man Rivers:
Tried to turn me into his eleven year old prostitute so that he could make on my back a ton of loot.
He would follow me up and down Main St., and act as if the post office was a fortuitous meet.

Old Man Rivers:
Tried to turn me into his eleven year old prostitute so that he could make from my spread legs a ton of loot.
He would whisper his dirtiness to me every chance he had, of how he wanted only to speak with me while in heat. And prepare me for the others he assumed I would meet, between the sheets.

Old Man Rivers:
Tried to turn me into his eleven year old prostitute so that he could make on my knees a ton of loot.
He, too, had two young daughters, but he dare not sin with his very own next of kin.

Old Man Rivers:
Tried to turn me into his eleven year old prostitute so that he could make from my rape a ton of loot.

He came a little too close that cold winter's day, and he received what he had been begging for, all of the loot in my child size boot.

Money for My Honey

Money for my honey, money for my honey;
Dear Sir, I'll take your money for my honey.
Money for my honey, money for my honey;
Dear Sir, I'm on sale today; just give me some money, for some of my sweet honey.
Money for my honey, money for my honey,
Dear Sir, I'm tired. I need to lay my head, even if it's on an old, unclean bed.
Money for my honey, money for my honey.
Dear Sir, I'll take your money for my honey.

The Reverend

It was just too much to have his heavy moans all over my bones.
So I ran away from home, just me and my red comb.
Yes, sir Reverend, this is my seventh night among the street lights.
Yes, sir, I'm on the streets both day and night.
Yes, Reverend, I'm afraid of who has me in his sights.
Yes, sir, I'm in need of a place to stay.

Yes, Reverend, it is hard to keep the perverts away.

Yes, sir, I understand: I a girl of 13 should get far away and learn all over how to play.

Yes, Reverend, I would love just to play. Oh ,yes, today is okay, but I'd like to tell my street sister if I may? Don't tell Kay? I see, for you molested her this past May.

Oh, Reverend, I didn't realize that your reference to play was for us to lay.

Oh, Reverend, please don't beg for me, okay? For your sinful request is much too heavy a price to pay on judgement day.

Dear Lord, I pray You advise the Reverend on his behavior this day. For he just might find himself on the streets one night, under this same dim light, desperately seeking to keep out of a pervert's sight.

No Beds Allowed

I don't do beds - For much too much has been said in those sinful beds.

I don't do beds - For much too much has gone on in those raping beds.

I don't do beds - For much too much has been denied in those wretched beds.

I don't do beds - For much too much death has occurred in those bloodstained beds.

I don't do beds - For much too much life has been wasted in those life—snatching beds.

I don't do beds - No linen necessary, any old wall is fine to catch a wink and stretch my spine, for this is how today my mind must rest.

Lisa C. Williams

I don't do beds, I don't do beds—for too many years of beatings, rapes, spoken words of death, and incestuous pregnancies and abortions have taken place in those baneful beds.

None of those beds are allowed in my house.

Inspired by the many women that surround.

No Longer

Dear God, I arise today through your strength;
Your love has added to my very being in yearly length:
No longer must I take shelter in just any old tent,
No longer must I beg for food only to be given a chewed piece of mint,
No longer must I feel compelled to go away or be sent,
No longer must I search for money only to find lent,
No longer must my mind be twisted and heavily bent,
No longer must my body be up for rent,
No longer must my soul feel totally spent,
No longer must I cry, for in spite of it all, my life was no accident: it was heavenly meant.

Purposed

Despite what you say, my life was no accident; it was heavenly inspired and purposely meant.

So know, by your devious actions, I will not be bent and my brain is not a space that your words of death may rent. Oh, no, my brother, my life was not an accident, I was uniquely created and purposely sent.

Chapter 3
Subjugation

SisterFriend

> Sisterfriend,
> Why does your mind bend?
> Yesterday we were neighboring as kin;
> Today you treat me silently as if I've sinned.
> Sisterfriend, look and admit how you've been altered since you welcomed him in.
> No longer are you allowed to smile, talk, think, or consider me or anyone else a friend.
> Sisterfriend, My Dear Sisterfriend, Why, Oh why, can't you see what is really happening?

Inspired by women in abusive and controlling relationships

Move On

> Exploring consciousness
> moves me to a joyful surge of tears
> as I no longer live in the painful sickness of fear.

Lisa C. Williams

Worthy

    I am worthy of all that is good,
Even if I feel God has deserted me.
I am worthy of all that is good,
Even when my self-worth walked out on me.
I am worthy of all that is good,
Even if my only love has fled from me.
I am worthy of all that is good,
Even when he chose another seductress over the children and me.
    I am worthy of all that is good,
Even when his choices are humiliating and tearing at me.
I am worthy of all that is good,
Even when he chooses to give all our money to her sexiness and allure of a promised good time.
    I am worthy of all that is good,
Even when his choices have put our safety and my mental health at risk.
    I am worthy of all that is good,
Even when my children are confused and hurting by his new priority.
    I am worthy of all that is good,
Even when his seductress, Crack, has me questioning all that I use to know.
    I am worthy of all that is good,
Even when I search myself for sin.
I am worthy of all that is good,
Even when I don't understand all that has been.
I am worthy of all that is good,
Even when it's hard to see through this time of betrayal.
I am worthy of all that is good,

Self Discovery

    Even when my thoughts and ways are not God's thoughts and ways.
    I am worthy of all that is good,
    Even when I must let go of the pain to see how with God he could change.
    I am worthy of all that is good, for my God has told me and blessed me so.

Inspired by an awe inspiring woman whose beauty shines through her strength

No More Light

    Of course I was forced.
    But you'd like to believe that on my own I would have received his seed and purposely conceived? Hmm.
    If this is what your mind believes, then you don't really know me, and I must question if you even like me. Clearly you're no friend of mine. I now must question all of mankind.
    Now get up and leave, before I believe this conversation is apart of his conspiracy.

    I thought he was my friend, but he too was in disguise as one of my incestuous kin.
    I faulted and fought myself all day long; oh, why wasn't I able to keep away his sin?
    He was my friend, only my friend, not a lover, but more like a protective brother.
    But that night, as darkness fell, I felt his dangerous touch; immediately I began to fight, but, Dear Lord, I couldn't overpower his might.

Searching my memory for what happened next, because today all I remember is that there was no more light. No more light.

It wasn't a date, so there is no date rape. It was simply plain and malicious rape. He acted like kin, you know, just a good brotherly friend. How asinine could I be for it was all just pretend; he had my body in his clutches to twist and perversely bend. Lord, I know it's wrong, but for today I do hate all men.

After he finished his sin—filled deed, he said with a smirk, "You got what you need." I lurched for him, focusing on amputating his not so private limb.
Do I call the police or not? Do I dress or not? Do I shower or not? Do I expose myself to ridicule or not? Do I question myself or not? Do I kill him or not? Do I go on living or not?

I find the pain and humiliation much too great, Lord, why can't I be stronger if I'm to endure this pain any longer?
My soul needs to make sure he never does this again, dawn the face of brotherly kin, in order to twist and bend and perpetrate his deadly sin. But for now I heed Your call for the adjusting of my sight. Your message was clear—that he would pay for his sinful touch. Oh, Lord, I thank You for the fleeting rest in your might, for in my nights, there is no more light, no more light.

No More Shade

My mother is *my* aunt's sister, and *my* aunt's husband is *my* father, hmm, figure it out yet? Why even bother.

They wanted to play, so they laid, and there in my aunt's house is where I, their second mistake, was made.

No more shade. No more shade. For all has been uncovered in the place where they laid.

Killed by Love

    He spoke with her,
    He smiled with her,
    He laughed with her,
    He cried with her,
    He walked with her,
    He made love with her,
    He courted her,
    He married her,
    He impregnated her,
    He cheated on her,
    He fathered her sister's child while married to her,
    He assaulted her,
    He beat her,
    He raped her,
    He murdered her,
    He decapitated her,
    He left her on the couch for *their* six children to find her,
    All of this in the name of loving her.

Inspired by ungovernable emotions and the truth of darkness

Lisa C. Williams

Truth

Live your truth even when others are living in denial.

Inspired by an awe inspiring and compassionate woman, Ms. Audrey L. Person.

Chapter 4

Façade

Mask

She smiles often,
but I can tell that her fragile inner mirrored shell is cracking.
She laughs often,
but I can tell that her tender seat of passion is crying.
She giggles often,
but I can tell that her delicate essence is barely coping.
She stares often,
but I can tell that her once alert impetus is now crashing.
She rocks often,
but I can tell never again will her soul be calm enough to be company.
She jabbers often,
but I can tell never again will she understand her uncontrollable chatter.
She smiles, laughs, giggles, stares, rocks, and jabbers no more. Her suffering forever closed.
She died before she ever lived. In the still of her silence, the pain finally ceased.

In memory of Bettie Mae Eldridge

Lisa C. Williams

Stepping Stones

Step out of the shadows of darkness, for the Lord awaits to illuminate your path of wholeness by His righteousness!

Inspired by Beautiful Stephanie of Apex

Hidden Rubies

Light cannot penetrate that which is hidden.

Inspired by Aunt Ruby

Undress

Undress your secrets so that you can heal by our Creator's will.

Inspired by Ann Smith

Once More

We rise slowly off our knees from praising the Lord,
only to speak with anger and total discord.
For we know not what we say or the price our words will cost someday.
Dear Lord, please have mercy, and forgive our words and bless our hearts once more,
prayerfully, before we are taken from this mortal shore.

Where is My God?

Where are You, God, where are You?
I'm searching my faith and work, but there's nothing to see of me in Your recorded ledger.
Where are You, God, where are You?
Do You take pleasure in my impecunious measure?
Where are You, God, where are You?
If not, then where is my promised treasure?
Where are You, God, where are You?

Stand

Lie down and I will rest my body upon your frame.
Stoop and I will wipe my boot upon your head.
Bend and I will sit my will upon your back.
Lean and I will hang my burdens upon your neck.
Stand upright and I will flee you.

Healing

Real healing only comes when you do an honest self examination and act upon ridding yourself of all the rubbish found concealed inside.

Freedom

I release all past abuse, anxiety, fear, failures, self-doubt, negative self- images, persecution, and hate. This day I surrender it all unto God.

Lisa C. Williams

Stand

Lie down and I will rest my body upon your frame.
Stoop and I will wipe my boot upon your head.
Bend and I will sit my will upon your back.
Lean and I will hang my burdens upon your neck.
Stand upright and I will flee you.

Beginning in the End

I awoke to understand:
that my God knew my needs and would provide for me,
the Mastermind who created my beginning by first creating my end.
Hmm, there was no more need to worry– only to trust, and, yes, begin
the journey that would allow God to have my heart fully on the mend.

Chapter 5

Saved

Travel

    I will illuminate the path on which you should travel.
    You, my dear, must adjust your attitude for the change in altitude.
    I will illuminate the path on which you should travel.
    You, my dear, must take off your heels and lace up your boots, for there are some low valleys and high hills along life's journey.
    I will illuminate the path on which you should travel.
    You, my dear, must today accept your karma, for others are waiting to get on with their travels.

Inspired by Soluria Pearson

Check Your Time

    I'm sorry, God, but I have no more time.
    I'll check my availability.
    I'll check my business schedule.
    I'll check my cluttered family calendar.

I'll check my date planner.
I'll check my email notes.
I'll check my first priority list.
I'll check my get—by—this—today calendar.
I'll check my palm pilot.
I'll check my schedule one last time, and see If I can fit You in tomorrow, for today I have no more time.

Oh, I didn't realize that You hadn't given any guarantee that I or tomorrow will even be.

Yes, that changes things. I will now check my internal self, for I must make time, I must make time. Right now for You, Lord, I must make time, because soon it will be my check-out time.

The invitation to follow Jesus has been extended to you—Romans 10:9.

God

God's Authority	~	Authors my life
God's Answer	~	Awakens my purpose
God's Back	~	Braces my fall
God's Boldness	~	Brings me life
God's Care	~	Checks my heart
God's Character	~	Creates my compassion
God's Eyes	~	Empowers my thoughts
God's Ears	~	Echoes my prayers
God's Hands	~	Handles me gently
God's Hair	~	Holds me together
God's Mouth	~	Matures my words
God's Mind	~	Molds my mind
God's Rod	~	Reproofs my actions

Self Discovery

God's Reach	~	Restores my faith
God's Spirit	~	Strengthens my steps
God's Shield	~	Shelters my soul
God's Tongue	~	Tempers my talk
God's Touch	~	Teaches me tenderness
God's Word	~	Washes me completely
God's Way	~	Welcomes me home

Inspired by Auntie

Birth

Creator of heaven and earth, You are the giver of my appointed birth.

Choose Life

Choose this day whom you will serve: God or your abuse?
Choose this day whom you will serve: God or your fear?
Choose this day whom you will serve: God or your pain?
Choose this day whom you will serve: God or your past?
Dear Lord, I choose this day life and to serve only You.

God's ABC

God:
Attitudes me
Breaks me
Comforts for me

Lisa C. Williams

Directs me
Empowers me
Fathers me
Guides me
Holds me
Jolts me
Knows me
Likes me
Matures me
Names me
Offers grace to me
Prepares me
Questions me
Reestablishes me
Silences me
Tutors me
Utilizes me
Values me
Warns me
Xeroxes me
Yields me
Zeros me to give me Zoë.

Comfort

Bathe	~	in God's truth,
Soak	~	in God's grace,
Rinse	~	in God's Spirit,
Dry	~	in God's Protection,
Dress	~	in God's Light, and
Mirror	~	in God's Holy Word.

Self Discovery

Life is…

    Awe inspired
    Blood flowing
    Calvary
    Dancing
    Evolving
    Full
    Giving
    Healthy
    Intense
    Joyful
    Kneeling
    Living
    Motion
    Nature
    Once
    Pure
    Questionable
    Respectful
    Salvation
    Teaching
    Unquenchable
    Voluptuous
    Water baptizing
    Xylophone
    Yearning
    Zoë

Lisa C. Williams

Assurance

Following His light assures your safety through the darkness.

Inspired by Marvin and Beverly Tucker

Unity

Yesterday I was:
United in suffering,
United in fear,
United in despair,
United in mourning,
United in hurt.
Today I am:
United in peace,
United in strength,
United in hope,
United in celebration,
United in healing,
For it is God who brought positive unity to my once chaotic and destructive life. Today, I honor God for unifying my life with the Holy Spirit!

Focus

If you just focused on the Lord, you could then see your life's possibilities, in pure and honest clarity.

Inspired by Soluria Pearson

Chapter 6

Praise

My Daily Prayer

Most Holy God, I glorify Your name and praise You for who You are and what You have done. You alone are holy and worthy of the highest praise. I honor You as the true and living God with all my heart, soul, mind and strength.

O, Gracious Lord, please shower Your grace on those I love who struggle with sin, who are broken by life's problems, plagued by disease, and caught in trying circumstances. I pledge to minister to their needs as I ask You to comfort, heal, strengthen, and mend in ways my words and deeds cannot.

Lord, thank You for hearing not only the prayer of my words, but the prayer of my heart. Be exalted in my life as I thank You for Your grace and mercy.

Through the power of the Holy Spirit and by the grace of Jesus, I offer this prayer. Amen

Inspired by an awesome woman of God, Mrs. Glenda Robinson.

Enlightenment

Don't allow yourself to be blinded by your own intrinsic light of introspection.
Seek divine guidance from Jesus Christ, the Son of God.
Don't allow yourself to be sidetracked by your own self-serving thoughts.
Seek divine discipline from Jesus Christ, the Son of God.
Don't allow yourself to be in disarray by your own slothfulness.
Seek divine order from Jesus Christ, the Son of God.
Don't allow yourself to be prideful by your own ego.
Seek divine acquiescence for all that you do from Jesus Christ, the Son of God.
Allow yourself to be immersed in the veracity of God's Light and your path will be forever illuminated.

Inspired by Auntie in all her wide hipped majesty! You live in me!

Powerless

Neglecting your personal communing time with the Lord will render you powerless.

My Savior!

It is My providence that has Me refilling your cup when it's empty,
For I am the giver of life, the Alpha and Omega.
It is My long suffering that has Me loving you so intensely,
For My life was given for yours, on Calvary.

It is My discipline that leads you through the valley of the shadow of death,
For I am thy Rod and thy Staff.
It is My stripes that provide for the healing of your hurt,
For I am that I am.
It is My walk that provides you illumination,
For I am the Way, the Truth, and the Light.
It is My covenant that has Me loving you as far as you can see,
For I have no end, I am Omnipotent.
Surely, Surely goodness and mercy has and will follow me all the days of my life.

This is my daily meditation along with the complete reading of Psalms 23.

Points of Entry

It's unacceptable to think and speak about an end
for your discovery of self has no end.
There are only new beginnings, starting lines, fresh starts, and points of entry.
A few detours are permitted along life's way, but they must first qualify as
purposeful pauses for gathering wisdom and dispensing lessons learned; Yields to lifelong
yearnings that allow you to sup from the enrichment of an overflowing cup, and
a forever point of entry that closes off to the past when it's time to meet your Savior.
Those are the only reasons, if you please. Ladies, excuses are not allowed so let them go.

Come with me and place in your memory that there are no U-turns or forever stops permitted along your way. In this space and time, this unique day once will you be.

For you are on the discovery of self that has no end.

That's why we must stand in awe at the treasures we'll uncover when we discover ourselves.

For there are no ends, only beginnings and points of entry.

Inspired by my sister-in-law Diana, written for Jackie Goodwyn.

Emancipation

Come when it will, My God listens for my pleas.
Come when it will, My God is equal to all my needs.
Come when it will, My God heals when I'm ill.
Come when it will, My God will provide all that shall be.
Come when it will, My God made promises just for me.
Come when it will, My God forgives, ensuring I will succeed.
Come when it will, My God will answer all.
When I say, "Oh, My God," please provide Your sweet release.

Inspired by an awesome woman of God, Mrs. Glenda Robinson.

Your Debt

You do owe a debt,
and that is the debt of release.
Speak and live your truth, so that others can see
My forgiveness and power is for all who have sinned in front of Me.

The Answer

    Stand with endurance for all that's unresolved in your life, and live your questions, for they must be.
    But for today, the questions shall be left unattended; they simply must be, if you're ever to fully realize Me.
    Stand with courage and live what your truth is now.
    Perhaps one day when the wheat is long and golden brown, and the light, sweet—smelling breeze mesmerizes your thoughts, you'll discover, by happenstance, that you are living your answer.

My daily creed for peace, rest and success!

Nightly Prayer

    Most Holy God, I bless Your name for who You are and what You have done.
    Father in heaven, I petition You right now in a special way.
    For You are the Creator of this earth, and the only giver of birth.
    I submit unto You every breath I take, each and every morning I wake.
    Forgive mymistakes, known and unknown, and cast them into that promised Forgotten Lake.
    Cast out anything that is not pleasing in Your sight, root out any unproductive thoughts, and remove any words of death that lurk just beneath my surface.
    I ask for You to wash my spirit and heal my soul with Your powerful balming touch, which has already done so much.

I'm grateful for being given this new merciful life lease, as I sup upon Your sweet anointed peace, and, yes, my thirst has been quenched by Your promised and delivered increase.

O, Gracious Lord, I close tonight on bent knees, asking to be restored and kept in full health both in my body and mind, so that I may continue to service mankind, through You until my time. Through the power of the Holy Spirit and by the grace of Jesus, I offer this prayer. Amen

Chapter 7
Melody

Spirituals

    Spirituals have an amazing way of :
Anointing your attitude;
Calming your castle;
Lessening your loss;
Mellowing your madness; and
Soothing your soul.
    Oh, how I love spirituals and their intrinsic value to heal the human spirit!

Dedicated to America: By God's grace and mercy we will heal our hurt from September 11, 2001, and rediscover and reaffirm our faith and strength as a people living in a truly blessed democracy.

Grace and Mercy

Dear Lord,
    Your grace and mercy have brought me through.
    Today I live each moment because of You.
    How do I thank You for saving a woman like me?

Your grace and mercy have brought me through;
Today I live in this moment because of You.
I want to thank You by giving and living my life for You.
Your grace and mercy have brought me through;
Today I live each moment because of You.
Society demanded that I should pay, but in You stepped and secured my stay.
Your grace and mercy have brought me through;
Today I live in this moment because of You.
I was blind, but now I see how You watched over me both day and night.
Your grace and mercy have brought me through;
Today I live in this moment only because of You!

It Is Well

It shall
be well,
and all shall
be well,
for It is well
within my soul.

My Soul

Yes, my God is real,
for I can feel Him deep down in my soul.
For my soul has been unsealed.
And today, I stand fully healed,
and obedient to God's everlasting will.

Self Discovery

Inspired by Ann Smith: may your light forever shine.

If I Can Help Some Woman

> If I can help some woman by my travels
> With a word or deed, then perhaps one day I'll make it home.
> If I can help some woman by my travels
> With kindness or a smile, then perhaps one day I'll make it home.
> If I can help some woman by my travels
> With a tune or prayer, then I perhaps one day I'll make it home.
> My travels were meant to help some woman, they were meant to help some woman,
> But if I can not help some woman, somewhere,
> then let me go on home, Dear Lord, so my living is not in vain.

Inspired by women wanting to be of good service to other women by using their gifts from the Lord.

Carolyn's Song

> She sings so heavenly.
> She sings so fervently.
> She sings so faithfully.
> She sings so our tender hearts will be healed.
> She sings so her purpose, too, will be fulfilled.

She sings: so full is her voice with God's praise and anointed grace.
She sings: so God's message of hope, healing, and forgiveness you, too, will taste.

Inspired by that awe inspiring earth moving songstress, Carolyn Sampson.

When She Sings

When she sings, fields of purple lilies sway and bow "hello."
When she sings, roaring rivers are peaceful with gentle flow.
When she sings, wind-swept meadows of wildflowers are all aglow.
When she sings, blue birds prance and dance in the sky.
When she sings, faith, hope and kindness spring up to grow, my, my.
When she sings, imperial waves become gentle as harbor bays.
When she sings, heavenly angels have much to say.
When she sings, our tuned ears rejoice at the gifted sound.
When she sings, healing, forgiveness, and celebration abound.
When she sings, hopeful words replace tears and fears.
When she sings, a baby's lullaby, it's an interlude to a peaceful night.

Inspired by an extraordinary woman of influence in song, Carolyn Sampson.

Chapter 8

Kindred

Marriage

> You and I are One,
> All of You and We are One.
> You and I are One,
> All of You and All of Me.
> Surely God meant for our marriage to be.

Inspired by an awesome marriage partnership between Lynn and Lisa!

Husband

> Husband, you make me feel as if I can:
> Dance as if no one is watching
> Love as if you're my first love affair
> Hope as if I've never been hurt before
> Sing as if I'm singing with a choir of angels, and
> Live as if the moon is my guide, the stars are my lights, and the breeze is my forever
> companion.

Lisa C. Williams

Laugh Out Loud

One might as well laugh, for life continues to get better with each passing day!

Inspired by the medicine Lisa takes daily!

Linkage

It must be love, for
we're linked
by our hearts and by our kinks.
And when my beautiful God—given man smiles and winks,
ah, my heart simply sinks.
It must be love, it must be love, because we're forever linked
by our hearts and by our kinks!

Essence of Life

My Dear Daughter,
your wombhood is the essence of life,
so be joyful and dance in your red flowing river,
for that new anointed life you are the appointed giver.

Paul, the Laughter in My Soul

Laughter, laughter on my lips!
Laughter, laughter on my large *swaying* hips!
Laughter, laughter at my table to dispense God's loving tips!

Self Discovery

    Paul is blackberry handsome, delightfully spirited, and laughter packed and sealed!
    Paul's life is pure, sweet laughter, raw and unmilled!
    Laughter, laughter morning and noon,
    Paul's laughter is brighter and more spectacular than the heavenly moon!

Inspired by my son Paul, a gift from God!

Joseph, My Joy

    Joy, Joy, my great Joy.
    Joy, Joy, down in my soul.
    Sweet Handsome, God Loving Joy.
    Joseph's birth was my God awakening Joy.
    Joseph, my Joy; Joseph, my Joy.
    I love you, Joseph, my Joy!

Inspired by my son Joseph!

Why

    Why do you walk with the chickens when you were given heavenly wings to fly with the eagles?

Inspired by my daughter Ashlyn!

Lisa C. Williams

Rest

    I pulled off my stockings and my dress, for it is time for needed rest.
    I pulled off my clothes, tied back my hair, and with patience washed all with care.
    I pulled off the covers, rejoicing that I'm free from the sweat of a lover.
    I pulled back the sheet, and fell to my knees: Oh, Lord bless me best, for it is time for needed rest.

Chapter 9

Friends

Friend

> My one true friend,
> is always there to help me mend,
> with God's Word when I have sinned.

She Knows Me

> She listens;
> She knows what's missing;
> She reads me, but
> She doesn't lead me;
> She gathers my many fragmented pieces, for
> She knows they'll need to be gingerly placed back together.
> For one day soon I'll say, Please, all is well; you may release me.
> So I can do all the wondrous things that God conceived for you and me."

Inspired by Sallie Abbas, Carol Brickhead, Carol Hunter, Carmen Jones, Rita Loyd, Soluria Pearson, Audrey Person and Carolyn Sampson.

Lisa C. Williams

Two Sisters

Here are two sisters name Frizz and Kink,
from our hearts there grows a link,
by our faith we sup a drink,
and our fears begin to shrink!

For Lisa, by Rita Loyd.

Two Sisters, Part II

We are linked, we're linked, yes, so heavenly linked,
our compassionate Lord has provided that sisterly link;
Yes, my dear sister we are so heavenly linked!
By our Lord's grace and mercy our fears will shrink!

Unhealthy

My brain
said no to the mental drain
of this unhealthy friendship train.
I place no blame; therefore, there is no shame.
It's just too much of a physical strain
for me to continue riding this unhealthy friendship train.

Chapter 10

Identity

Pureness of Love

It is pure joy to love yourself, more than any other person possibly could!

Hues of Skin

My skin is dark, and it's the living color of bark.
Many have laughed at my dark, for they say I'm not pretty nor cute,
since I'm not lightly toasted almond, high yellow, or caramel butter cream.
What can I say: they're too blind to see, that not with any old sand did God make me.
God used the deepest and darkest hues of earth, to ensure I would have a strong and healthy birth.
For my skin is dark, and it's the living color of bark.
I love my dark, for it is God's loving owner's mark!

Lisa C. Williams

Little Black Dress

I wore that black dress, because it made me look like I had less. Oh, what a mess; if I really had less, I could dress with the best, and burn that *not* so little black dress.

Black Hair

Bald
Corn Rolled
Curled
Frizzed
Finger Waved
French Braid
Glued
Locks
Natural
Nappy
Plaited
Permed
Twisted
Sewn
Straighten
Wrapped
Weaved
Wigged
Whatever the hairdo, we are forever sisters for we are linked, by our glorious kinks!

Chapter 11
Self

Celebrating Life

> I will bring myself,
> you will bring yourself,
> they will bring themselves,
> and together we will all be ourselves
> in a circle of friends, celebrating life!

Inspired by Rita Loyd's "Celebration" painting that adorns my first book, *A Circle of Friends: Celebrating Life.*

Celebration

I celebrate my God in praise and song for what has been done.
I celebrate my history that will be created from this day on.
I celebrate my independent thoughts and choices.
I celebrate my responsible actions when it comes to my life and those I love.

I celebrate my mental health by staying focused on God's Word.

I celebrate my ability to say "no" without feeling guilty.

I celebrate my positive attitude by keeping negative thoughts and folks out of my space.

I celebrate my sisters who have exposed their hurt in order to heal.

I celebrate my *own* discovery of self.

I celebrate my new life with a circle of friends!

Self Trust

Listen to yourself and trust yourself to do what is right; today you are responsible for your own awareness, choices, and actions. Trust yourself to do what is right and then do it! Self trust is the one gift you must give to yourself.

Inspired by my friend, Carol.

Peace

Discover yourself today,
share your truths tomorrow.
For your truths will speak life—changing freedom
and peace for another sisters' painful yesterday.

Self Discovery Affirmation

Searching for meaning, searching for worth, I am directed inward.

Self Discovery

I excavate the layers of resentment,
guilt, sadness, and shame
to find that my identity is none of these emotions
but a beautiful spirit that waits just beneath.
Buried beneath the tiers of buried tears,
I am discovering the unique facets of my spirit being.
Quietly she has waited for the rage of the ego to subside,
for her voice is gentle
and is not easily heard over the rant.

"Self Discovery" affirmation, by Rita Loyd.

Standing In the Gap

She is a child who finds her answers in God's Word—when her secrets were unearthed her hurt was healed.

She is a woman who uses her healing to comfort and quietly push other women to unearth their secrets so they too can heal their hurt, learn forgiveness, and live what they're purposed for.

She is a wife who uses her purpose to nurture, strengthen, and bring peace, laughter, and joy to her husband.

She is a mother who uses her life to nurture, strengthen, love, and provide safety and guidance for her children, so that they will one day touch other's with their truth and laughter.

She is a sister who uses gentle truths to stand in the gap for the sole purpose of teaching others about hope, healing, humility and honor in living their truth.

Inspired by Auntie and the gentle nudge from Dr. Johnnie Miles.

Lisa C. Williams

My Vow

My past will not live in my future.

Discovery of Self

I am beautiful and in awe of the essence of life I have uncovered!
My discovery of self is a wonderful delight in my Savior's sight!
Praises, Lord, for protecting me through those dubious years with Your awesome might!
Blessings, Lord, for guiding my discovery of self into Your Light!

About the Author

Lisa Williams, a native of Long Island, New York, after enduring years of mental, physical, sexual abuse and neglect, was abandoned at the age of twelve years old and homeless at seventeen. Nevertheless, she has turn tragedy into triumph, obstacles into opportunities, and challenges into channels of hope for herself and others. Today, Lisa dramatically touches the lives of women with her story of abuse, hope and victory.

Self Discovery

Williams' not-for-profit organization (The Center for H.O.P.E.) has been the vehicle for moving hundreds of women each year toward self-discovery and financial freedom. She speaks loudly and stands boldly in the gap for others so that they can one day stand in the sunshine and celebrate life.

Today, Williams is an inspirational speaker whose seminars are designed to motivate people to action. Her national lecture circuit and media appearances cover topics on:

>Building Positive Attitudes
>Goal Setting and Prioritizing
>Overcoming the Bondage of Abuse
>Living a Financially Healthy Life
>Getting Prepared for Your Future Mate
>Effective Parenting Skills, and
>Succeeding in Business

The outgrowth of her financial seminars "Becoming Debt Free," "Creating Wealth," and "Family Finances" have led to appearances on local and state-wide television talk programs and national radio. Williams financial planning book, *Living in the Black—Brings Financial Health, Wealth and Independence* will be available Spring 2002.

Williams' inspirational story has been told in two books, *A Circle of Friends Celebrating Life* and *Self Discovery Prose and Poems: A Journey from Pain to Purpose*. Also, *A Circle of Friends* CD has been released as a tool of reflection, mediation and enlightenment for those experiencing the pain of neglect and abuse.

Williams is a wife to her best friend, Lynn Calvo, and mother of a fusion of five biological and adopted children. In 1999, all under the age of 9, the children were the youngest entrepreneurs in North Carolina. They opened P&J Sweet Treats, Inc., a bakery business that was enormously successful their very first year of business! P&J Sweet Treats continues to grow as they refine their bakery business and give generously back to their community! Visit P&J Sweet Treats e-commerce store at www.pjsweettreats.com.

Lisa believes, the keys to living a rewarding and financially healthy life are attitude, education, and action. "Attitude is everything!" she's quick to explain. "It dictates what we can expect from life. If I can affect a positive change in the way people are thinking about themselves and their finances, then I have fertile ground to plant seeds for financial health, wealth and independence." Today, Lisa speaks and travels around the world as author, inspirational speaker and financial motivator.

For information on scheduling speaking engagements, contact:
The Center for H.O.P.E.
919.468.9884
center4hope@nc.rr.com
www.center4hope@nc.rr.com

Appendix A

Purposeful Scriptures

The following scriptures have provided nourishment and guidance for my daily living. They too can help you in each experience.

What to do when you are—

Afraid, Angry, Unsure About God, Ashamed, and Have Doubt about Yourself

What to do when you are feeling—

Guilty, Confused, Worried, Stressed & Anxious, Lonely, and Discouraged

What to do when you—

Feel everything is going wrong in your life, Are deserted by friends and family, Are Facing trying circumstances, Want to forgive, and Want to live as God would have it.

The following scriptures are a compilation of the women's personal favorites. All scriptures contained here are taken from New Living Translation (NLT) Bible.

Self Discovery

What to do when you are:

Afraid

2 Timothy 1—Read Chapter
1:7
For God has not given us a spirit of fear and timidity, but of power, love, and self-discipline.
Psalms 23—Read Chapter
23:4
Even when I walk through the dark valley of death, I will not be afraid, for you are close beside me. Your rod and your staff protect and comfort me.
23:5
You prepare a feast for me in the presence of my enemies. You welcome me as a guest, anointing my head with oil. My cup overflows with blessings.
Psalms 27—Read Chapter
27:1
A psalm of David. The Lord is my light and my salvation—so why should I be afraid? The LORD protects me from danger—so why should I tremble?
27:2
When evil people come to destroy me, when my enemies and foes attack me, they will stumble and fall.
27:3
Though a mighty army surrounds me, my heart will know no fear. Even if they attack me, I remain confident.
Psalms 31—Read Chapter
31:24
So be strong and take courage, all you who put your hope in the Lord!

Psalms 56—Read Chapter
56:11
I trust in God, so why should I be afraid? What can mere mortals do to me?
Psalms 91—Read Chapter
91:10
No evil will conquer you; no plague will come near your dwelling.
91:11
For he orders his angels to protect you wherever you go.
91:14
The LORD says, "I will rescue those who love me. I will protect those who trust in my name."
Proverbs 3 Read Chapter
3:25
You need not be afraid of disaster or the destruction that comes upon the wicked,
3:26
for the Lord is your security. He will keep your foot from being caught in a trap.
1 John—4 Read Chapter
4:18
Such love has no fear because perfect love expels all fear. If we are afraid, it is for fear of judgment, and this shows that his love has not been perfected in us.
John 14—Read Chapter
14:27
"I am leaving you with a gift—peace of mind and heart. And the peace I give isn't like the peace the world gives. So don't be troubled or afraid."
Romans 8—Read Chapter
8:31
What can we say about such wonderful things as these? If God is for us, who can ever be against us?

8:35
Can anything ever separate us from Christ's love? Does it mean he no longer loves us if we have trouble or calamity, or are persecuted, or are hungry or cold or in danger or threatened with death?
8:36
"For your sake we are killed every day; we are being slaughtered like sheep."
8:37
No, despite all these things, overwhelming victory is ours through Christ, who loved us.
8:38
And I am convinced that nothing can ever separate us from his love. Death can't, and life can't. The angels can't, and the demons can't. Our fears for today, our worries about tomorrow, and even the powers of hell can't keep God's love away.
8:39
Whether we are high above the sky or in the deepest ocean, nothing in all creation will ever be able to separate us from the love of God that is revealed in Christ Jesus, our Lord.

Angry

James 1—Read Chapter
1:19
My dear brothers and sisters, be quick to listen, slow to speak, and slow to get angry.
1:20
Your anger can never make things right in God's sight.
Ephesians 4—Read Chapter
4:26
And "don't sin by letting anger gain control over you." Don't let the sun go down while you are still angry.

4:31
Get rid of all bitterness, rage, anger, harsh words, and slander, as well as all types of malicious behavior.
4:32
Instead, be kind to each other, tenderhearted, forgiving one another, just as God through Christ has forgiven you.
Proverbs 14—Read Chapter
14:16
The wise are cautious and avoid danger; fools plunge ahead with great confidence.
14:17
Those who are short-tempered do foolish things, and schemers are hated.
15:1
A gentle answer turns away wrath, but harsh words stir up anger.
16:32
It is better to be patient than powerful; it is better to have self-control than to conquer a city.
25:21
If your enemies are hungry, give them food to eat. If they are thirsty, give them water to drink.
25:22
You will heap burning coals on their heads, and the Lord will reward you.
Ecclesiastic 7—Read Chapter
7:9
Don't be quick-tempered, for anger is the friend of fools.
Romans 12—Read Chapter
12:19
Dear friends, never avenge yourselves. Leave that to God. For it is written, "I will take vengeance; I will repay those who deserve it," says the Lord.

Matthew 6—Read Chapter
6:14
"If you forgive those who sin against you, your heavenly Father will forgive you.

Unsure About God

Mark 11—Read Chapter
11:22
Then Jesus said to the disciples, "Have faith in God.
11:23
I assure you that you can say to this mountain, 'May God lift you up and throw you into the sea,' and your command will be obeyed. All that's required is that you really believe and do not doubt in your heart.
11:24
Listen to me! You can pray for anything, and if you believe, you will have it.
11:25
But when you are praying, first forgive anyone you are holding a grudge against, so that your Father in heaven will forgive your sins, too.
Isaiah 46—Read Chapter
46:10
Only I can tell you what is going to happen even before it happens. Everything I plan will come to pass, for I do whatever I wish.
46:11
I will call a swift bird of prey from the east—a leader from a distant land who will come and do my bidding. I have said I would do it, and I will.
Isaiah 54—Read Chapter
54:10
"For the mountains may depart and the hills disappear, but even then I will remain loyal to you. My covenant of blessing will never be broken," says the LORD, who has mercy on you.

1 Peter 4—Read Chapter
4:12
Dear friends, don't be surprised at the fiery trials you are going through, as if something strange were happening to you.
4:13
Instead, be very glad—because these trials will make you partners with Christ in his suffering, and afterward you will have the wonderful joy of sharing his glory when it is displayed to all the world.
4:14
Be happy if you are insulted for being a Christian, for then the glorious Spirit of God will come upon you.
2 Peter 3—Read Chapter
3:9
The Lord isn't really being slow about his promise to return, as some people think. No, he is being patient for your sake. He does not want anyone to perish, so he is giving more time for everyone to repent.
Matthew 9—Read Chapter
9:1
Jesus climbed into a boat and went back across the lake to his own town.
9:2
Some people brought to him a paralyzed man on a mat. Seeing their faith, Jesus said to the paralyzed man, "Take heart, son! Your sins are forgiven."
9:3
"Blasphemy! This man talks like he is God!" some of the teachers of religious law said among themselves.
9:4
Jesus knew what they were thinking, so he asked them, "Why are you thinking such evil thoughts?
9:5
Is it easier to say, 'Your sins are forgiven' or 'Get up and walk'?

Self Discovery

9:6
I will prove that I, the Son of Man, have the authority on earth to forgive sins." Then Jesus turned to the paralyzed man and said, "Stand up, take your mat, and go on home, because you are healed!"

9:7
And the man jumped up and went home!

9:18
As Jesus was saying this, the leader of a synagogue came and knelt down before him. "My daughter has just died," he said, "but you can bring her back to life again if you just come and lay your hand upon her."

9:19
As Jesus and the disciples were going to the official's home,

9:20
a woman who had had a hemorrhage for twelve years came up behind him. She touched the fringe of his robe,

9:21
for she thought, "If I can just touch his robe, I will be healed."

9:22
Jesus turned around and said to her, "Daughter, be encouraged! Your faith has made you well." And the woman was healed at that moment.

9:23
When Jesus arrived at the official's home, he noticed the noisy crowds and heard the funeral music.

9:24
He said, "Go away, for the girl isn't dead; she's only asleep." But the crowd laughed at him.

9:25
When the crowd was finally outside, Jesus went in and took the girl by the hand, and she stood up!

Ashamed

Isaiah 50—Read Chapter
50:7
Because the Sovereign LORD helps me, I will not be dismayed. Therefore, I have set my face like a stone, determined to do his will. And I know that I will triumph
2 Timothy—1 Read Chapter
2 Timothy 1:8
So you must never be ashamed to tell others about our Lord. And don't be ashamed of me, either, even though I'm in prison for Christ. With the strength God gives you, be ready to suffer with me for the proclamation of the Good News.
I turned away from God, but then I was sorry. I kicked myself for my stupidity! I was thoroughly ashamed of all I did in my younger days.
2Timothy—2:15
Work hard so God can approve you. Be a good worker, one who does not need to be ashamed and who correctly explains the word of truth.

Having Doubts About Yourself

Philippians 4—Read Chapter
4:6
Don't worry about anything; instead, pray about everything. Tell God what you need, and thank him for all he has done.
41:10
Don't be afraid, for I am with you. Do not be dismayed, for I am your God. I will strengthen you. I will help you. I will uphold you with my victorious right hand.
43:2
When you go through deep waters and great trouble, I will be with you. When you go through rivers of difficulty, you will not drown! When

you walk through the fire of oppression, you will not be burned up; the flames will not consume you.
Proverbs 3—Read Chapter
3:5
Trust in the LORD with all your heart; do not depend on your own understanding.
Proverbs 29—Read Chapter
29:18
When people do not accept divine guidance, they run wild. But whoever obeys the law is happy.
Psalms 106—Read Chapter
106:3
Happy are those who deal justly with others and always do what is right.
Psalms 147—Read Chapter
147:3
He heals the brokenhearted, binding up their wounds.
2 Corinthians 1—Read Chapter
1:3
All praise to the God and Father of our Lord Jesus Christ. He is the source of every mercy and the God who comforts us.
1:4
He comforts us in all our troubles so that we can comfort others. When others are troubled, we will be able to give them the same comfort God has given us.
Isaiah 43—Read Chapter
43:2
When you go through deep waters and great trouble, I will be with you. When you go through rivers of difficulty, you will not drown! When you walk through the fire of oppression, you will not be burned up; the flames will not consume you.

Lisa C. Williams

What to do when you are feeling:

Guilty

Isaiah 43—Read Chapter
43:25
"I—yes, I alone—am the one who blots out your sins for my own sake and will never think of them again."
55:7
Let the people turn from their wicked deeds. Let them banish from their minds the very thought of doing wrong! Let them turn to the Lord that he may have mercy on them. Yes, turn to our God, for he will abundantly pardon.
1 John 1—Read Chapter
1:9
But if we confess our sins to him, he is faithful and just to forgive us and to cleanse us from every wrong.
John 5—Read Chapter
5:24
"I assure you, those who listen to my message and believe in God who sent me have eternal life. They will never be condemned for their sins, but they have already passed from death into life.
John 8—Read Chapter
8:10
Then Jesus stood up again and said to her, "Where are your accusers? Didn't even one of them condemn you?"
8:11
"No, Lord," she said. And Jesus said, "Neither do I. Go and sin no more."
2 Corinthians 5—Read Chapter
5:17

What this means is that those who become Christians become new persons. They are not the same anymore, for the old life is gone. A new life has begun!
Hebrews 10—Read Chapter
10:22
Let us go right into the presence of God, with true hearts fully trusting him. For our evil consciences have been sprinkled with Christ's blood to make us clean, and our bodies have been washed with pure water.

Confused

1 Corinthians 14—Read Chapter
14:33
For God is not a God of disorder but of peace, as in all the other churches.
1 Peter 4—Read Chapter
4:12
Dear friends, don't be surprised at the fiery trials you are going through, as if something strange were happening to you.
4:13
Instead, be very glad—because these trials will make you partners with Christ in his suffering, and afterward you will have the wonderful joy of sharing his glory when it is displayed to all the world.
Psalms 32—Read Chapter
32:8
The Lord says, "I will guide you along the best pathway for your life. I will advise you and watch over you."
Proverbs 3—Read Chapter
3:5
Trust in the Lord with all your heart; do not depend on your own understanding.
Isaiah 30—Read Chapter

30:21
And you will hear a voice say, "This is the way; turn around and walk here."
James 3—Read Chapter
3:16
For wherever there is jealousy and selfish ambition, there you will find disorder and every kind of evil.
3:17
But the wisdom that comes from heaven is first of all pure. It is also peace loving, gentle at all times, and willing to yield to others. It is full of mercy and good deeds. It shows no partiality and is always sincere.
3:18
And those who are peacemakers will plant seeds of peace and reap a harvest of goodness.

Worried

Philippians 4—Read Chapter
4:6
Don't worry about anything; instead, pray about everything. Tell God what you need, and thank him for all he has done.
4:7
If you do this, you will experience God's peace, which is far more wonderful than the human mind can understand. His peace will guard your hearts and minds as you live in Christ Jesus.
4:8
And now, dear brothers and sisters, let me say one more thing as I close this letter. Fix your thoughts on what is true and honorable and right. Think about things that are pure and lovely and admirable. Think about things that are excellent and worthy of praise.
Psalms 55—Read Chapter
55:22

Self Discovery

Give your burdens to the Lord, and he will take care of you. He will not permit the godly to slip and fall.
55:23
But you, O God, will send the wicked down to the pit of destruction. Murderers and liars will die young, but I am trusting you to save me.
1 Peter 5—Read Chapter
5:7
Give all your worries and cares to God, for he cares about what happens to you.
Matthew 6—Read Chapter
6:25
"So I tell you, don't worry about everyday life—whether you have enough food, drink, and clothes. Doesn't life consist of more than food and clothing?"
6:26
"Look at the birds. They don't need to plant or harvest or put food in barns because your heavenly Father feeds them. And you are far more valuable to him than they are."
6:27
"Can all your worries add a single moment to your life? Of course not."
6:28
"And why worry about your clothes? Look at the lilies and how they grow. They don't work or make their clothing,"
6:29
"Yet Solomon in all his glory was not dressed as beautifully as they are."
6:30
"And if God cares so wonderfully for flowers that are here today and gone tomorrow, won't he more surely care for you? You have so little faith!"
6:31
"So don't worry about having enough food or drink or clothing."

6:32
"Why be like the pagans who are so deeply concerned about these things? Your heavenly Father already knows all your needs,"
6:33
"And he will give you all you need from day to day if you live for him and make the Kingdom of God your primary concern."
John 14—Read Chapter
14:1
"Don't be troubled. You trust God, now trust in me."
Isaiah 41 Read Chapter
41:10
Don't be afraid, for I am with you. Do not be dismayed, for I am your God. I will strengthen you. I will help you. I will uphold you with my victorious right hand.

Stressed & Anxious

Hebrews 12—Read Chapter
12:1
Therefore, since we are surrounded by such a huge crowd of witnesses to the life of faith, let us strip off every weight that slows us down, especially the sin that so easily hinders our progress. And let us run with endurance the race that God has set before us.
Romans 5—Read Chapter
5:3
We can rejoice, too, when we run into problems and trials, for we know that they are good for us—they help us learn to endure.
5:4
And endurance develops strength of character in us, and character strengthens our confident expectation of salvation.
5:5

Self Discovery

And this expectation will not disappoint us. For we know how dearly God loves us, because he has given us the Holy Spirit to fill our hearts with his love.

Romans 8—Read Chapter

8:25
But if we look forward to something we don't have yet, we must wait patiently and confidently.

8:26
And the Holy Spirit helps us in our distress. For we don't even know what we should pray for, nor how we should pray. But the Holy Spirit prays for us with groanings that cannot be expressed in words.

Psalms 27—Read Chapter

27:14
Wait patiently for the Lord. Be brave and courageous. Yes, wait patiently for the LORD.

Psalms 37—Read Chapter

37:7
Be still in the presence of the Lord, and wait patiently for him to act. Don't worry about evil people who prosper or fret about their wicked schemes.

37:8
Stop your anger! Turn from your rage! Do not envy others—it only leads to harm.

37:16
It is better to be godly and have little than to be evil and possess much.

James 1—Read Chapter

1:2
Dear brothers and sisters, whenever trouble comes your way, let it be an opportunity for joy.

1:3
For when your faith is tested, your endurance has a chance to grow.

1:4

So let it grow, for when your endurance is fully developed, you will be strong in character and ready for anything

Lonely

John 14—Read Chapter
14:8
Philip said, "Lord, show us the Father and we will be satisfied."
Deuteronomy 4—Read Chapter
4:31
For the LORD your God is merciful—he will not abandon you or destroy you or forget the solemn covenant he made with your ancestors.
Deuteronomy 31—Read Chapter
31:6
"Be strong and courageous! Do not be afraid of them! The Lord your God will go ahead of you. He will neither fail you nor forsake you."
Romans 8—Read Chapter
8:35
Can anything ever separate us from Christ's love? Does it mean he no longer loves us if we have trouble or calamity, or are persecuted, or are hungry or cold or in danger or threatened with death?
8:36
"For your sake we are killed every day; we are being slaughtered like sheep."
8:37
No, despite all these things, overwhelming victory is ours through Christ, who loved us.
8:38
And I am convinced that nothing can ever separate us from his love. Death can't, and life can't. The angels can't, and the demons can't. Our fears for today, our worries about tomorrow, and even the powers of hell can't keep God's love away.

8:39
Whether we are high above the sky or in the deepest ocean, nothing in all creation will ever be able to separate us from the love of God that is revealed in Christ Jesus our Lord.
Psalms 46—Read Chapter
46:1
God is our refuge and strength, always ready to help in times of trouble.

Discouraged

John 14—Read Chapter
14:27
"I am leaving you with a gift—peace of mind and heart. And the peace I give isn't like the peace the world gives. So don't be troubled or afraid."
Psalms 27—Read Chapter
27:1
A psalm of David. The Lord is my light and my salvation—so why should I be afraid? The Lord protects me from danger—so why should I tremble?
27:2
When evil people come to destroy me, when my enemies and foes attack me, they will stumble and fall.
27:3
Though a mighty army surrounds me, my heart will know no fear. Even if they attack me, I remain confident.
27:4
The one thing I ask of the Lord—the thing I seek most—is to live in the house of the Lord all the days of my life, delighting in the Lord's perfection and meditating in his Temple.
27:5
For he will conceal me there when troubles come; he will hide me in his sanctuary. He will place me out of reach on a high rock.

27:6
Then I will hold my head high, above my enemies who surround me. At his Tabernacle I will offer sacrifices with shouts of joy, singing and praising the LORD with music.
27:7
Listen to my pleading, O Lord. Be merciful and answer me!
27:8
My heart has heard you say, "Come and talk with me." And my heart responds, "LORD, I am coming."
27:9
Do not hide yourself from me. Do not reject your servant in anger. You have always been my helper. Don't leave me now; don't abandon me, O God, of my salvation!
27:10
Even if my father and mother abandon me, the Lord will hold me close.
27:11
Teach me how to live, O Lord. Lead me along the path of honesty, for my enemies are waiting for me to fall.
27:12
Do not let me fall into their hands. For they accuse me of things I've never done and breathe out violence against me.
27:13
Yet I am confident that I will see the Lord's goodness while I am here in the land of the living.
27:14
Wait patiently for the Lord. Be brave and courageous. Yes, wait patiently for the LORD.
Galatians 6—Read Chapter
6:9
So don't get tired of doing what is good. Don't get discouraged and give up, for we will reap a harvest of blessing at the appropriate time.
John 14—Read Chapter

Self Discovery

14:27
"I am leaving you with a gift—peace of mind and heart. And the peace I give isn't like the peace the world gives. So don't be troubled or afraid."
2 Corinthians 4—Read Chapter
4:8
We are pressed on every side by troubles, but we are not crushed and broken. We are perplexed, but we don't give up and quit.
4:9
We are hunted down, but God never abandons us. We get knocked down, but we get up again and keep going.
Hebrews 10—Read Chapter
10:35-36
Do not throw away this confident trust in the Lord, no matter what happens. Remember the great reward it brings you!
Patient endurance is what you need now, so you will continue to do God's will. Then you will receive all that he has promised.

What to do when you:

Feel everything is going wrong in your life

Hebrews 10—Read Chapter
10:23
Without wavering, let us hold tightly to the hope we say we have, for God can be trusted to keep his promise.
Hebrews 11—Read Chapter
11:1
What is faith? It is the confident assurance that what we hope for is going to happen. It is the evidence of things we cannot yet see.
Habakkuk 2—Read Chapter

2:3
But these things I plan won't happen right away. Slowly, steadily, surely, the time approaches when the vision will be fulfilled. If it seems slow, wait patiently, for it will surely take place. It will not be delayed.

Psalms 27—Read Chapter

27:14
Wait patiently for the Lord. Be brave and courageous. Yes, wait patiently for the LORD.

Isaiah 25—Read Chapter

25:9
In that day the people will proclaim, "This is our God. We trusted in him, and he saved us. This is the Lord, in whom we trusted. Let us rejoice in the salvation he brings!"

Romans 13—Read Chapter

13:13
We should be decent and true in everything we do, so that everyone can approve of our behavior. Don't participate in wild parties and getting drunk, or in adultery and immoral living, or in fighting and jealousy.

13:14
But let the Lord Jesus Christ take control of you, and don't think of ways to indulge your evil desires.

Are Deserted by friends and family

2 Corinthians 4—Read Chapter

4:9
We are hunted down, but God never abandons us. We get knocked down, but we get up again and keep going.

Isaiah 49—Read Chapter

49:15

"Never! Can a mother forget her nursing child? Can she feel no love for a child she has borne? But even if that were possible, I would not forget you!"
49:16
"See, I have written your name on my hand. Ever before me is a picture of Jerusalem's walls in ruins."
1 Peter 5—Read Chapter
5:7
Give all your worries and cares to God, for he cares about what happens to you.

Are Facing Trying circumstances

Philippians 4—Read Chapter
4:6
Don't worry about anything; instead, pray about everything. Tell God what you need, and thank him for all he has done.
4:7
If you do this, you will experience God's peace, which is far more wonderful than the human mind can understand. His peace will guard your hearts and minds as you live in Christ Jesus.
Nahum 1—Read Chapter
1:7
The Lord is good. When trouble comes, he is a strong refuge. And he knows everyone who trusts in him.
Isaiah 42 Read Chapter
42:16
I will lead blind Israel down a new path, guiding them along an unfamiliar way. I will make the darkness bright before them and smooth out the road ahead of them. Yes, I will indeed do these things; I will not forsake them.
Hebrews 11—Read Chapter

11:1
What is faith? It is the confident assurance that what we hope for is going to happen. It is the evidence of things we cannot yet see.

Want to forgive

Matthew 5—Read Chapter
5:10
God blesses those who are persecuted because they live for God, for the Kingdom of Heaven is theirs.
5:11
"God blesses you when you are mocked and persecuted and lied about because you are my followers."
5:12
"Be happy about it! Be very glad! For a great reward awaits you in heaven. And remember, the ancient prophets were persecuted, too."
Matthew 6—Read Chapter
6:14
"If you forgive those who sin against you, your heavenly Father will forgive you."
6:15
"But if you refuse to forgive others, your Father will not forgive your sins."
1 Peter 2—Read Chapter
2:19
For God is pleased with you when, for the sake of your conscience, you patiently endure unfair treatment.
2:20
Of course, you get no credit for being patient if you are beaten for doing wrong. But if you suffer for doing right and are patient beneath the blows, God is pleased with you.
2:21

Self Discovery

This suffering is all part of what God has called you to. Christ, who suffered for you, is your example. Follow in his steps.
2:22
He never sinned, and he never deceived anyone.
2:23
He did not retaliate when he was insulted. When he suffered, he did not threaten to get even. He left his case in the hands of God, who always judges fairly.
1 Peter 3—Read Chapter
3:9
Don't repay evil for evil. Don't retaliate when people say unkind things about you. Instead, pay them back with a blessing. That is what God wants you to do, and he will bless you for it.
3:10
For the Scriptures say, "If you want a happy life and good days, keep your tongue from speaking evil, and keep your lips from telling lies."
1 Peter 4—Read Chapter
4:12
Dear friends, don't be surprised at the fiery trials you are going through, as if something strange were happening to you.
4:13
Instead, be very glad—because these trials will make you partners with Christ in his suffering, and afterward you will have the wonderful joy of sharing his glory when it is displayed to all the world.
4:14
Be happy if you are insulted for being a Christian, for then the glorious Spirit of God will come upon you.
Philippians 3 Read Chapter
3:13
No, dear brothers and sisters, I am still not all I should be, but I am focusing all my energies on this one thing: Forgetting the past and looking forward to what lies ahead,

3:14
I strain to reach the end of the race and receive the prize for which God, through Christ Jesus, is calling us up to heaven.

Want to live as God would have it

Joshua 1—Read Chapter
1:8
Study this Book of the Law continually. Meditate on it day and night so you may be sure to obey all that is written in it. Only then will you succeed.
1:9
"I command you—be strong and courageous! Do not be afraid or discouraged. For the Lord your God is with you wherever you go."
1 Thessalonians 4 Read Chapter
4:3
God wants you to be holy, so you should keep clear of all sexual sin.
4:4
Then each of you will control your body and live in holiness and honor
1 Thessalonians 5—Read This Chapter
5:16
Always be joyful.
5:17
Keep on praying.
5:18
No matter what happens, always be thankful, for this is God's will for you who belong to Christ Jesus.
Isaiah 30—Read Chapter
30:21
And you will hear a voice say, "This is the way; turn around and walk here."
Isaiah 48—Read Chapter

Self Discovery

48:17
"The Lord, your Redeemer, the Holy One of Israel, says: I am the LORD your God, who teaches you what is good and leads you along the paths you should follow."
Isaiah 58—Read Chapter
58:11
The LORD will guide you continually, watering your life when you are dry and keeping you healthy, too. You will be like a well-watered garden, like an ever-flowing spring.
Deuteronomy 6—Read Chapter
6:4
"Hear, O Israel! The Lord is our God, the Lord alone.
6:5
And you must love the Lord your God with all your heart, all your soul, and all your strength.
6:6
And you must commit yourselves wholeheartedly to these commands I am giving you today.
6:7
Repeat them again and again to your children. Talk about them when you are at home and when you are away on a journey, when you are lying down and when you are getting up again.
6:8
Tie them to your hands as a reminder, and wear them on your forehead.
6:9
Write them on the door posts of your house and on your gates.
Romans 8—Read Chapter
8:14
For all who are led by the Spirit of God are children of God.
Romans 12—Read Chapter
12:1

And so, dear brothers and sisters, I plead with you to give your bodies to God. Let them be a living and holy sacrifice—the kind he will accept. When you think of what he has done for you, is this too much to ask?
12:2
Don't copy the behavior and customs of this world, but let God transform you into a new person by changing the way you think. Then you will know what God wants you to do, and you will know how good and pleasing and perfect God's Will really is.

Appendix B

Learned Lessons

In this journey to healing, my relationship with Jesus Christ has been the sustaining force. For years I tried to overcome on my own, but it became clear that if I was to overcome my past I had to act upon my trust and faith in Jesus Christ. When I changed my way of thinking, my old life gradually died and was replaced with a new and joyous one.

The following quotes are from the lessons learned along my journey. They have challenged my attitude and resolve for peaceful and successful living. They too can help you, as you, take the first step toward walking your own path to healing.

Getting Your Priorities Straight

- Focus first always on God.
- Bless and praise God daily.
- Present all concerns and problems to God through prayer.
- Trust God enough to work out your trying circumstances, especially when you can't naturally see the solution.

- Read, meditate, and study God's Word both day and night.
- Surround yourself with truly wise people who have demonstrated their close walk with God, and who believe in the power of prayer.
- Enjoy serving the Lord.
- Tell others about God, but allow your actions to speak even louder about God's goodness in your life.

Attitude is Everything

- It dictates what we can expect from life. It can affect a positive change in the way people are thinking about themselves and their circumstances. A positive attitude is the fertile ground necessary for God to plant seeds of hope, healing, forgiveness, and prosperity.
- A relaxed and positive attitude lengthens life, but a negative attitude robs you of life.
- Your attitude impacts other as well as determines the extent of happiness and success your children will experience.
- Reading The Word daily will keep your mind and attitude refreshed and focused on God, which is good.

Improving Behavior

- Get rid of anger, rage, resentment, and the need to punish. These things only serve to promote negative and destructive behavior that can never be healthy.
- Other's will seek your company when your behavior is pleasing, and new and positive things will enter into your life.

- Your children's behavior will improve when yours does.

Trusting God

- When I can not see the logic in my place in life, I must trust that God has me there for a reason, and I will seek to learn a new life lesson.
- When one door closes, I trust that the correct door will open that I am to enter safely.
- I trust in God and not in myself, for God knew my end from the beginning.
- I will no longer play the "what—ifs" or the "if-only" games, for they only seek to sabotage God's plans for my life. I'll make decisions and choices based on my prayer, God's Word, and God's guidance.
- My daily interactions with God build my trust.
- God challenges me in my daily walk so that my trust in Him can mature.

Living Your Purpose

- Learn God's voice and know His call so you won't miss the opportunity to fulfill the purpose for your life; for we all have been purposed for a particular job to do that only we can do.
- Fulfilling God's purpose for your life isn't about you but about the many people who will be touched and led to God by your obedience.
- Surrendering to God will impact your life like nothing else will.

- God will not call you to do something you're not prepared for, but remember your preparation is yours.
- Everything that has happened in your life both good and bad has prepared you for your Purpose.

Leaning on Faith

- Faith allows us to get up every morning when the world throws dirt on top of your casket.
- Faith makes the everyday impossible—possible.
- Faith allows me to surrender my all to a God I can not see.
- Faith defies science.
- Faith allows me to go from being homeless to being a home owner.
- Faith is believing in the power of God, who created the moon that controls the tide.

Appendix C

Resources For Healing the Hurt

The following pages contain resources for assisting you with immediate protection, counseling, shelter, crisis intervention, and self discovery.

If you are in a violent situation please pick up the phone and call for assistance now.

National Domestic Violence Hotline
1-800-799-SAFE (7233
1-800-787-3224 (TDD)

The Rape, Abuse, Incest National Network (RAINN) will automatically transfer you to the rape crisis center nearest you, anywhere in the nation. It can be used as a last resort if people cannot find a domestic violence shelter. 1-800-656-HOPE

National Domestic
Violence Hotline
1-800-799-SAFE (7233)
1-800-787-3224 (TDD)

State Coalitions on Domestic Violence
Alabama Coalition Against Domestic Violence
P.O. Box 4762
Montgomery, AL 36101
1-800-650-6522

Alaska Network on Domestic Violence and Sexual Assault
    130 Seward Street, Room 209
    Juneau, AK 99801
    Phone: 907-586-3650
    FAX: 907-463-4493

Arizona Coalition Against Domestic Violence
    100 West Camelback Road, Suite 109
    Phoenix, AZ 85013
    Phone: 602-279-2900
    FAX: 602-279-2980
    E-mail: acadv@goodnet.com

Arkansas Coalition Against Domestic Violence
    #1 Sheriff Lane, Suite C
    North Little Rock, AR 72114
    Phone: 501-812-0571
    FAX: 501-812-0578
    E-mail: ssigmon@arkansas.net

Coalition to End Domestic and Sexual Violence
    2064 Eastman Ave., Suite 104
    Ventura, CA 93003
    Phone: 805-654-8141
    FAX: 805-654-1264
    24-Hour Hotline: 805-656-1111
    Spanish Hotline: 800-300-2181
    TDD: 805-656-4439

Statewide California Coalition for Battered Women
    3711 Long Beach Blvs. Suite 718
    Long Beach CA 90807
    Toll-Free: 888-SCCBW-52
    Phone: 562-981-1202
    Fax: 562-981-3202
    E-mail: sccbw@sccbw.org

Colorado Domestic Violence Coalition
    P.O. Box 18902
    Denver, CO 80218
    TOLL-FREE: 888-778-7091
    Phone: 303-831-9632
    FAX: 303-832-7067
    E-mail: ccadv@ix.netcom.com

D.C. Coalition Against Domestic Violence
    513 U Street NW
    Washington, DC 20001
    Phone: 202-783-5332
    FAX: 202-387-5684

My Sister's Place
    P.O. Box 29596
    Washington, DC 20017
    24-hour hotline: 202-529-5991
    Administrative Office: 202-529-5261

Delaware Coalition Against Domestic Violence
    P.O. Box 847
    Wilmington, DE 19899
    Phone: 302-658-2958
    FAX: 302-658-5049
    Hotlines by Counties:
    24-hour bilingual line: 888-LAC-C571 (888-522-2571)
    New Castle: 302-762-6110
    Kent & Sussex: 302-422-8058

Florida Coalition Against Domestic Violence
    308 East Park Avenue
    Tallahassee, FL 32301
    TOLL-FREE: 800-500-1119
    Phone: 850-425-2749
    FAX: 850-425-3091

Georgia Advocates for Battered Women and Children
　　250 Georgia Avenue, SE, Suite 308
　　Atlanta, GA 30312
　　TOLL-FREE: 800-334-2836
　　Phone: 404-524-3847
　　FAX: 404-524-5959
Hawaii State Coalition Against Domestic Violence
　　98-939 Moanalua Road
　　Aiea, HI 96701-5012
　　Phone: 808-486-5072
　　FAX: 808-486-5169
Iowa Coalition Against Domestic Violence
　　2603 Bell Avenue, Suite 100
　　Des Moines, IA 50321
　　TOLL-FREE: 800-942-0333
　　Phone: 515-244-8028
　　FAX: 515-244-7417
Idaho Coalition Against Sexual and Domestic Violence
　　815 Park Blvd, Suite 140
　　Boise, ID 83712
　　TOLL-FREE: 888-293-6118
　　Phone: 208-384-0419
　　FAX: 208-331-0687
　　E-mail: domvio@micron.net
Illinois Coalition Against Domestic Violence
　　801 South 11th Street
　　Springfield, Illinois 62703
　　Phone: 217-789-2830
　　FAX: 217-789-1939
　　E-mail: ilcadv@springnet1.com

Friends of Battered Women and Their Children
    P. O. Box 5185
    Evanston, IL 60204
    Phone: 773-274-5232
    FAX: 773-274-2214
    HOTLINE: 1-800-603-HELP
    E-mail:info@afriendsplace.org

Life Span
    P.O. Box 445
    Des Plaines IL 60016
    24-Hour Crisis Line: 847-824-4454
    Phone: 847-824-0382
    Fax: 847-824-5311
    E-mail: life-span@life-span.org
    Special site on Police Domestic Violence

Indiana Coalition Against Domestic Violence
    2511 E. 46th Street, Suite N-3
    Indianapolis, IN 46205
    TOLL-FREE: 800-332-7385
    Phone: 317-543-3908
    FAX: 317-377-7050

Kansas Coalition Against Sexual and Domestic Violence
    820 SE Quincy, Suite 600
    Topeka, KS 66612
    TOLL-FREE: 888-END-ABUSE (Kansas state-wide hotline)
    Phone: 785-232-9784
    FAX: 785-232-9937

Kentucky Domestic Violence Association
    P.O. Box 356
    Frankfort, KY 40602
    Phone: 502-875-4132
    FAX: 502-875-4268

Louisiana Coalition Against Domestic Violence
    P.O. Box 77308
    Baton Rouge, LA 70879-7308
    Phone: 225-752-1296
    FAX: 225-751-8927
Maine Coalition to End Domestic Violence
    128 Main Street
    Bangor, ME 04401
    Phone: 207-941-1194
    FAX: 207-941-2327
Maryland Network Against Domestic Violence
    6911 Laurel Bowie Road, Suite 309
    Bowie, MD 20715
    TOLL-FREE: 800-MD-HELPS
    Phone: 301-352-4574
    FAX: 301-809-0422
Jane Doe Inc./Massachusetts Coalition Against Sexual Assault and Domestic Violence
    14 Beacon Street, Suite 507
    Boston, MA 02108
    Phone: 617-248-0922
    FAX: 617-248-0902
Bay County Women's Center
    P.O. Box 1458
    Bay City, MI 48706
    TOLL-FREE: 800-834-2098
    Phone: 517-686-4551
    FAX: 517-686-0906
    Michigan 24-Hour Crisis Line: 517-265-6776
Minnesota Coalition for Battered Women
    450 North Syndicate Street, Suite 122
    St. Paul, MN 55104

　　　　Metro-Area Hotline: 651-646-0994
　　　　Phone: 651-646-6177
　　　　FAX: 651-646-1527
　　　　E-mail: mcbw@pclink.com
Missouri Coalition Against Domestic Violence
　　　　415 E. McCarty Street
　　　　Jefferson City, MO 65101
　　　　Phone: 573-634-4161
　　　　FAX: 573-636-3728
Women's Support and Community Services
　　　　2838 Olive St.
　　　　St. Louis, MO 63103
　　　　HOTLINE: 314-531-2003
　　　　Office: 314-531-9100
Mississippi State Coalition Against Domestic Violence
　　　　P.O. Box 4703
　　　　Jackson, MS 39296-4703
　　　　TOLL-FREE: 800-898-3234
　　　　Phone: 601-981-9196
　　　　FAX: 601-981-2501
　　　　E-mail: mcadv@misnet.com
Crisis Line
　　　　P.O. Box 6644
　　　　Great Falls, MT 59406
　　　　Phone: 406-453-HELP
　　　　TOLL-FREE: 1-888-587-0199
Montana Coalition Against Domestic and Sexual Violence
　　　　P.O. Box 633
　　　　Helena, MT 59624
　　　　Phone: 406-443-7794
　　　　FAX: 406-443-7818

Nebraska Domestic Violence and Sexual Assault Coalition
825 M Street, Suite 404
Lincoln, NE 68508-2253
TOLL-FREE: 800-876-6238
Phone: 402-476-6256
FAX: 402-476-6806

Nevada Network Against Domestic Violence
100 West Grove, Suite 315
Reno, NV 89509
TOLL-FREE: 800-500-1556
Phone: 775-828-1115
FAX: 775-828-9991

SAFE House
18 Sunrise Drive, Ste. G-70
Henderson, NV 89014
Phone: 702-451-4203
FAX: 702-451-4302
E-mail: safe@intermind.net

New Hampshire Coalition Against Domestic and Sexual Violence
P.O. Box 353
Concord, NH 03302-0353
TOLL-FREE: 800-852-3388 (in New Hampshire)
Helpline: 603-225-9000 (outside of New Hampshire)
Phone: 603-224-8893
Fax: 603-228-6096

New Jersey Coalition for Battered Women
2620 Whitehorse/Hamilton Square Road
Trenton, NJ 08690
TOLL-FREE: for Battered Lesbians: 800-224-0211 (in NJ only)
Phone: 609-584-8107
FAX: 609-584-9750
TTY: 609-584-0027 (9am-5pm, then into message service)

Strengthen Our Sisters
    P.O. Box U
    Hewitt, NJ 07421
    E-mail: ssisters@warwick.net
    24-Hour Hotline: 973-728-0007
New Mexico State Coalition Against Domestic Violence
    P.O. Box 25266
    Albuquerque, NM 87125
    TOLL-FREE: 800-773-3645 (in New Mexico Only)
    Legal Helpline: 800-209-DVLH
    Phone: 505-246-9240
    FAX: 505-246-9434
    E-mail: nmcadv@nmcadv.org
New York State Coalition Against Domestic Violence
    79 Central Avenue
    Albany, NY 12206
    TOLL-FREE: 800-942-6906
    Phone: 518-432-4864
    FAX: 518-463-3155
North Carolina Coalition Against Domestic Violence
    301 W. Main Street
    Durham, NC 27701
    Phone: 919-956-9124
    FAX: 919-682-1449
INTERACT
        Serving Victims and Survivors of Domestic Violence and Sexual Assault
    612 Wade Avenue
    Raleigh, NC 27605
    Phone: 919-828-7501
    FAX: 919-828-8304
    24 Hour Phone Lines

Rape and Sexual Assault Services 919-828-3005
Domestic Violence Services 919-828-7740
North Dakota Council on Abused Women's Services
State Networking Office
418 East Rosser Avenue, Suite 320
Bismarck, ND 58501
TOLL-FREE: 800-472-2911 (In ND Only)
Phone: 701-255-6240
FAX: 701-255-1904
Ohio Domestic Violence Network
4041 North High Street, Suite 400
Columbus, OH 43214
TOLL-FREE: 800-934-9840
Phone: 614-784-0023
FAX: 614-784-0033
Oklahoma Coalition Against Domestic Violence and Sexual Assault
2525 NW Expressway, Suite 208
Oklahoma City, OK 73116
TOLL-FREE: 800-522-9054
Phone: 405-848-1815
FAX: 405-848-3469
Oregon Coalition Against Domestic and Sexual Violence
520 NW Davis, Suite 310
Portland, OR 97209
TOLL-FREE: 800-622-3782
Phone: 503-223-7411
FAX: 503-223-7490
Pennsylvania Coalition Against Domestic Violence/National Resource Center on Domestic Violence
6440 Flank Drive, Suite 1300
Harrisburg, PA 17112-2778
TOLL-FREE: 800-932-4632

Phone: 717-545-6400
FAX: 717-545-9456
Pennsylvania Coalition Against Rape
125 N. Enola Drive
Enola PA 17025
HOTLINE: 800-692-7445
Phone: 717-728-9740
Fax: 717-728-9781
TTY: 877-585-1091
E-Mail: Stop@pcar.org
Women's Center of Montgomery County
Main Administrative Office:
101 Washington Lane, Ste. WC-1
Jenkintown PA 19046
Toll-free hotline: 800-773-2424
Norristown Office:
Women's Advocacy Project
400 Courthouse Plaza, 18 W. Airy St
Norristown PA 19404
610-279-1548
Pottstown Office:
Women's Advocacy Project
555 High Street, 2nd Floor
Pottstown PA 19464
610-970-7363
Laurel House
P.O. Box 764
Norristown, PA 19404
Phone: 800-642-3150
HOTLINE: 1-800-642-3150
Fax: 610-275-4018
E-Mail: LaurelHaus@aol.com

Rhode Island Coalition Against Domestic Violence
    422 Post Road, Suite 202
    Warwick, RI 02888
    TOLL-FREE: 800-494-8100
    Phone: 401-467-9940
    FAX: 401-467-9943

South Carolina Coalition Against Domestic Violence & Sexual Assault
    P.O. Box 7776
    Columbia, SC 29202-7776
    TOLL-FREE: 800-260-9293
    Phone: 803-256-2900
    FAX: 803-256-1030

South Dakota Coalition Against Domestic Violence and Sexual Assault
    P.O. Box 141
    Pierre, SD 57501
    TOLL-FREE: 800-572-9196
    Phone: 605-945-0869
    FAX: 605-945-0870

South Dakota Network Against Family Violence and Sexual Assault
    1-800-430-SAFE

Resource Center of Aberdeen, S.D
    24-Hour Crisis Line: (605) 226-1212
    Toll Free: (888) 290-2935

Tennessee Task Force Against Domestic Violence
    P.O. Box 120972
    Nashville, TN 37212
    TOLL-FREE: 800-356-6767
    Phone: 615-386-9406
    FAX: 615-383-2967

Texas Council on Family Violence
    P.O. Box 161810
    Austin, TX 78716

TOLL-FREE: 800-525-1978
Phone: 512-794-1133
FAX: 512-794-1199
Families In Crisis, Inc.
P.O. Box 25
Killeen, Texas 76540
(254) 634-1184
1-888-799-SAFE
Domestic Violence Advisory Council
120 North 200 West
Salt Lake City, UT 84103
TOLL-FREE: 800-897-LINK
Phone: 801-538-4100
FAX: 801-538-3993
Women Helping Battered Women
Phone: 802-658-1996
Toll-free: 1-800-228-7395
Women's Rape Crisis Center
1-800-489-7273
Vermont Network Against Domestic Violence and Sexual Assault
P.O. Box 405
Montpelier, VT 05601
Phone: 802-223-1302
FAX: 802-223-6943
E-mail: vnadvsa@sover.net
Virginians Family Violence and Sexual Assault Hotline
2850 Sandy Bay Road, Suite 101
Williamsburg, VA 23185
TOLL-FREE: 800-838-VADV
Phone: 757-221-0990
FAX: 757-229-1553

Washington State Coalition Against Domestic Violence
    8645 Martin Way NE - Suite 103
    Lacey, WA 98516
    E-mail: wscadv@cco.net
    Phone: 360-407-0756
    FAX: 360-407-0761
    TTY: 360-407-0767

Washington State Domestic Violence Hotline
    Tel: 800-562-6025
    E-mail: csn@willapabay.org

West Virginia Coalition Against Domestic Violence
    Elk Office Center
    4710 Chimney Drive, Suite A
    Charleston, WV 25302
    Phone: 304-965-3552
    FAX: 304-965-3572

Manitowoc Domestic Violence Center
    PO Box 1142
    Manitowoc, WI 54220
    Phone: 920-684-5770

Wisconsin Coalition Against Domestic Violence
    1400 East Washington Avenue, Suite 232
    Madison, WI 53703
    Phone: 608-255-0539
    FAX: 608-255-3560

Wyoming Coalition Against Domestic Violence and Sexual Assault
    P.O. Box 236
    Laramie, WY 82073
    TOLL-FREE: 800-990-3877
    Phone: 307-755-5481
    FAX: 307-755-5482

National Organizations
- Family Violence Prevention Fund
  383 Rhode Island Street, Suite 304
  San Francisco, CA 94103-5133
  Phone: 415-252-8900
  FAX: 415-252-8991
- National Coalition Against Domestic Violence
  Policy Office
  P.O. Box 34103
  Washington, DC 20043-4103
  Phone: 703-765-0339
  FAX: 202-628-4899
- National Coalition Against Domestic Violence
  P.O. Box 18749
  Denver, CO 80218
  Phone: 303-839-1852
  FAX: 303-831-9251
- National Battered Women's Law Project
  275 7th Avenue, Suite 1206
  New York, NY 10001
  Phone: 212-741-9480
  FAX: 212-741-6438
- Victim Services
  Domestic Violence Shelter Tour
  2 Lafayette Street
  New York, NY 10007
  Phone: 212-577-7700
  Fax: 212-385-0331
  24-hour hotline: 800-621-HOPE (4673)

National Resource Center On DV
    Pennsylvania Coalition Against Domestic Violence
    6400 Flank Drive, Suite 1300
    Harrisburg, PA 17112
    Phone: 800-537-2238
    FAX: 717-545-9456
Health Resource Center on Domestic Violence
    Family Violence Prevention Fund
    383 Rhode Island Street, Suite 304
    San Francisco, CA 94103-5133
    Phone: 800-313-1310
    FAX: 415-252-8991
Battered Women's Justice Project
    Minnesota Program Development, Inc.
    4032 Chicago Avenue South
    Minneapolis, MN 55407
    TOLL-FREE: 800-903-0111 Ext: 1
    Phone: 612-824-8768
    FAX: 612-824-8965
Resource Center on Domestic Violence, Child Protection, and Custody
    NCJFCJ
    P.O. Box 8970
    Reno, NV 89507
    Phone: 800-527-3223
    FAX: 775-784-6160
    They are only a resource center for professionals and agencies.
Battered Women's Justice Project
    c/o National Clearinghouse for the Defense of Battered Women
    125 South 9th Street, Suite 302
    Philadelphia, PA 19107

TOLL-FREE: 800-903-0111 ext. 3
Phone: 215-351-0010
FAX: 215-351-0779
National Clearinghouse is a national resource and advocacy center providing assistance to women defendants, their defense attorneys, and other members of their defense teams in an effort to insure justice for battered women charged with crimes.

National Clearinghouse on Marital and Date Rape
2325 Oak Street
Berkeley, CA 94708
Phone: 510-524-1582

Center for the Prevention of Sexual and Domestic Violence
936 North 34th Street, Suite 200
Seattle, WA 98103
Phone: 206-634-1903
FAX: 206-634-0115

National Network to End Domestic Violence - Administrative Office
c/o Texas Council on Family Violence
P.O. Box 161810
Austin, TX 78716
Phone: 512-794-1133
FAX: 512-794-1199

National Network to End Domestic Violence
666 Pennsylvania Avenue SE, Suite 303
Washington, DC 20003
Phone: 202-543-5566
FAX: 202-543-5626

Crisis Hotline Phone Numbers
This list is provided as a resource for youth workers. Inclusion on this list does service agencies and ministries.

Abuse:
National On Child Abuse/Neglect 800-FYI-3366

Self Discovery

Childhelp 800-422-4453
AIDS:
CDC National Aids Hotline 800-342-AIDS
The above in Spanish 800-344-7432
National HIV/AIDS Teen Hotline (Fri. & Sat. 6:30 p.m.-12:00 a.m.) 800-440-8336
Alcohol:
Children of Alcoholics Foundation 800-359-2623
Mothers Against Drunk Driving 800-438-6233
Students Against Drunk Driving 508-481-3568
Blindness:
American Foundation for the Blind 800-232-5463
Cults:
Cult Hotline (Mercy House) 606-748-9961
Hearing/Deafness:
Better Hearing Institute 800-327-9355
Dial A Hearing Screening Test 800-222-3277
Drugs:
American Council for Drug Education 800-488-3784
Cocaine Hotline 800-262-2463
National Institute on Drug Abuse Helpline 800-662-4357
National Recovery Institute 800-442-7623
Eating Disorders:
National Association of Anorexia Nervosa 847-831-3438
National Anorexic Aid Society 614-436-1112
Overeaters Anonymous Hotline 505-891-2664
Education:
National GED Information Hotline 800-626-9433
Employment:
Job Corps 800-733-5627
Gambling:
Compulsive Gambling Hotline 410-332-0402

Health:
National STD Line 800-227-8922
Orton Dyslexia Society 800-222-3123
Shriners Hospital Referral Line 800-237-5055
Housing/Homelessness:
HUD Housing Discrimination Hotline 800-669-9777
National Coalition for the Homeless 202-737-6444
Incest:
Survivors of Incest Anonymous (over 18) 410-282-3400
Literacy:
National Literacy Hotline 800-228-8813
Mental Health:
Depression Awareness Recognition 800-421-4211
Oaks Treatment Center 800-843-6257
Missing Children:
Child Find of America 800-426-5678
Missing Children Help Center 800-872-5437
Pregnancy:
Bethany Lifeline Pregnancy Hotline 800-238-4269
Rape:
RAINN-Rape Abuse Incest Nat. Network 800-656-4673
Crime & Rape Victim Hotline 212-577-7777
Runaway:
Boystown National Hotline 800-448-3000
Covenant House Nineline 800-999-9999
Laurel House 714-832-0207
National Runaway Switch Board 800-621-4000
Self Help:
Shoplifters Alternative 800-848-9595
Nicotine Anonymous 877-879-6422

Self Discovery

If there's a problem with a listing, a number that has changed, or you'd like to recommend a contact, please e-mail us at *center4hope@nc.rr.com*. Thanks!

0-595-20162-8